REAL WORLD MATH: Personal Finance

Using Credit Wisely

KATIE MARSICO

Published in the United States of America by Cherry Lake Publishing
Ann Arbor, Michigan
www.cherrylakepublishing.com

Math Education: Dr. Timothy Whiteford, Associate Professor of Education at St. Michael's College
Financial Adviser: Kenneth Klooster, financial adviser at Edward Jones Investments
Reading Adviser: Marla Conn, ReadAbility, Inc.

Photo Credits: © Andresr/Shutterstock Images, cover, 1, 13; © Mikhail hoboton Popov/Shutterstock Images, 5; © Andy Dean Photography/Shutterstock Images, 6; © Ryan McVay/Thinkstock.com, 9; © BernardaSv/Thinkstock.com, 11; © baranq/Shutterstock Images, 15; © Antonio_Diaz/iStock.com, 17; © Jupiterimages/Thinkstock.com, 18; © kali9/iStock.com, 21; © Phartisan | Dreamstime.com - Tow-truck Picking Up Broken Down Car Photo, 23; © Ryan R Fox/Shutterstock Images, 24; © ronstik/Shutterstock Images, 27; © danielfela/Shutterstock Images, 28

Library of Congress Cataloging-in-Publication Data

Marsico, Katie, 1980-
    Using credit wisely / Katie Marsico.
  pages cm. — (Real world math: personal finance)
  Includes bibliographical references and index.
  ISBN 978-1-63362-578-5 (hardcover) — ISBN 978-1-63362-758-1 (pdf) —
  ISBN 978-1-63362-668-3 (pbk.) — ISBN 978-1-63362-848-9 (ebook)
  1. Consumer credit—Juvenile literature. 2. Credit cards—Juvenile literature. 3. Finance, Personal—Juvenile literature. 4. Mathematics—Juvenile literature. I. Title.

  HG3755.M3225 2016
  332.7'43—dc23   2015008968

Cherry Lake Publishing would like to acknowledge the work of
the Partnership for 21st Century Skills. Please visit *www.p21.org*
for more information.

Printed in the United States of America
Corporate Graphics

ABOUT THE AUTHOR

Katie Marsico is the author of more than 200 children's books. She lives in a suburb of Chicago, Illinois, with her husband and children.

TABLE OF CONTENTS

Who's Paying for Your Purchase?

Javier wants to buy a new computer but doesn't have enough money. Luckily, Javier's big brother, Luis, offers to let him borrow whatever he needs. In return, Luis expects Javier to pay him back in three months—and wash his car every weekend. Javier agrees and heads to the computer store!

Here, Luis is the lender, or creditor, and Javier is the borrower. Javier is using **credit** to get his computer. The amount Javier borrows is called the **principal**.

When you buy something on credit, someone else

If you borrow money from family members, you might have to pay them back with more than just cash.

loans you money to pay for your purchase. Of course, you're expected to pay back everything that you owe. But the lender is taking a risk that you won't do this. So, credit purchases usually involve an additional payment above and beyond the money that goes toward the principal. This compensates lenders for the risk they're taking. For Luis, the additional payment is having Javier wash his car.

Unlike Luis, however, banks aren't going to ask you to wash cars! Instead, they'll charge you **interest**, or an

*When a family buys a house, they usually will
need to borrow money and pay it back slowly.*

21ST CENTURY CONTENT

It's important to think ahead before using credit to make a purchase. For example, let's say your parents borrow $100,000 at 6 percent interest to buy a house. By the time the loan is completely repaid in 30 years, they'll have paid the bank $215,838. The total interest will be more than the amount they originally borrowed!

additional amount of money added to the loan. It's typically calculated as a percentage of the money you've borrowed. In most cases, people make a monthly payment to creditors. It includes part of the principal plus interest. You pay interest only on the principal you still owe.

Every time you borrow money, it is reported to a credit bureau. Credit bureaus are businesses that create credit reports on everyone who is paying off debts. If you repay your loans on time, you get a good credit rating. If you don't, you get a bad credit rating. Banks and other companies that you've asked to loan you money often check your credit rating before saying yes. If you have good credit, you're more likely to appear **trustworthy**—and to be a good candidate for a loan.

CHAPTER 2

DIFFERENT KINDS OF CREDIT

Dara's family needs a new refrigerator. They go to a department store and pick out a model that costs $1,619.99, including tax. They can't afford to pay the entire amount right away though. Instead, they will make their purchase with credit. They have two choices—use a credit card or get an **installment loan**.

Banks issue credit cards. You've probably seen people use them at the store. At the checkout counter, either the cashier or the customer swipes the credit card through a machine. This machine confirms that the credit card is **valid**. Then the buyer signs a **receipt**, and the purchase is complete. No actual cash changes hands.

When you charge something to a credit card, you are asking the bank to temporarily pay for what you bought. Then, once a month, you get a bill that lists all the

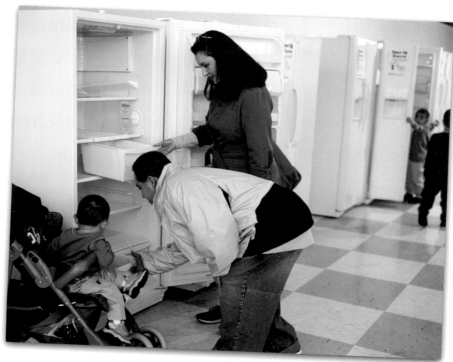

Refrigerators are expensive. People often need loans to buy them.

Real World Math Challenge

Jessie and her older sister, Mia, are using Mia's new credit card to shop at the mall. Together, they purchase four outfits for $135.48. Then they buy sunglasses for their dad for $19.99. Other purchases include art supplies for $13.47 and three CDs for $16.97 each.

- How much of Mia's $500.00 credit limit remains?

(Turn to page 30 for the answers)

But what if Dara's family doesn't want to use a credit card to buy their refrigerator? Depending on the store's policy, it's possible they'll be able to apply for an installment loan. With an installment loan, the lender gives the borrower cash for a one-time purchase. The borrower then repays the lender in monthly amounts that also include interest. Installment loans are typically used for major purchases such as cars, appliances, and home repairs.

What else do you need to know if you rely on credit to go shopping? There are several important guidelines that will help you use credit wisely. Keep reading to learn what financial choices are best for boosting your credit rating!

People who use credit cards need to understand how they work.

CHAPTER 3

Do the Math: Using a Credit Card

Credit cards serve an important purpose. Sometimes people need or want to make a purchase right away. But they may not have all the money to pay for it at that moment. Credit cards allow someone to shop without having to worry about making a full payment up front.

Still, owning and using a credit card is a big responsibility. Some people are tempted to buy whatever they want whenever they want it. But purchasing something simply because you are able to isn't necessarily good for your finances—or your credit rating. Remember that every time you charge a purchase to your credit card, you're asking the bank to buy it for you. Eventually, it's your responsibility to repay the bank.

If you don't pay your bills right away, the interest on them can really add up.

Not repaying creditors or not repaying them on time often has serious consequences. In many cases, banks will raise your interest rate or charge other penalties. If they decide you're not using your card responsibly, it's possible that they'll lower your credit limit. Just as importantly, it's likely that your credit rating will also suffer. Ultimately, this affects how much other creditors are willing to lend you and how much interest you'll have to pay.

LIFE AND CAREER SKILLS

Some banks issue special prepaid credit cards to younger customers. This involves an adult transferring money out of his or her checking account and onto the prepaid card. This way, everything you buy with the card has already been paid for. Prepaid credit cards often help people learn how to avoid spending more than they can afford.

A prepaid card is a good option for younger shoppers.

You may feel like you can afford something, but do the math first.

For these reasons, it's always smart to think ahead whenever you use your credit card to make a purchase. Will you be able to repay the bank the minimum monthly amounts required? What if it takes more than a few months to repay everything in full? In some cases, people decide it's better to pay with cash or wait until a big item goes on sale.

Of course, if you're responsible, you'll be able to make credit cards work for you, rather than against you. Planning ahead and buying only what you can afford will help you build a good credit history. Also, be sure to pay creditors regularly and on time. Ideally, try to pay off your balance every month in order to avoid interest charges.

Now you know more about the risks and responsibilities that go hand in hand with using credit cards. Next, it's time to focus on making the best choices if you're considering an installment loan.

REAL WORLD MATH CHALLENGE

Patrick's dad buys him a mountain bike that costs $449.99, plus 7 percent sales tax. Patrick plans to repay Dad $20.00 each week.

- How much sales tax is charged on the bike?
- How long will it take Patrick to repay Dad in full?

(Turn to page 30 for the answers)

Do the Math: Installment Loans

Ethan goes with his cousin Lucy to buy a new car from a local dealership. The cost of the automobile is $30,000. Lucy puts a down payment of $5,000 on the car, but she's still responsible for the remaining $25,000.

Fortunately, the dealership offers installment loans. For expensive, one-time purchases, it's often more practical to pay with an installment loan than a credit card. Installment loans also tend to involve a longer repayment period. That's why the interest rate is generally lower for installment loans than most credit cards.

When most people buy cars, they make multiple payments over time.

Depending on the type of purchase you're making, it's possible that you'll be able to shop around for an installment loan. Several types of businesses provide them to people hoping to borrow money. These include banks, car dealerships, mortgage brokers, and department stores. Based on a person's credit rating, such businesses sometimes offer competitive interest rates.

For example, banks compete with one another for customers. That's why it often helps to talk to loan officers at different banks in your community. They decide who does or doesn't get to borrow money. This way, you're more likely to have a wider variety of loan options to choose from.

Much like using a credit card, taking out an installment loan involves making a commitment, or a promise. Regardless of what business is willing to lend you money, you're still expected to repay the loan. If you fail to do so—or fail to pay according to the **terms** of your loan agreement—the lender will take action. Sometimes this means a **penalty** that's added on to your next monthly payment. In other cases, it involves a raised interest rate. And, in certain situations, lenders will even repossess, or take back, your purchase.

Let's say Lucy fails to make multiple payments on the new car she just bought. It's possible that the lender who provided her with an installment loan will take the car back. In addition, Lucy will have damaged her credit rating in the process.

If you never pay your debts, the bank can take back the item it loaned you money to buy.

An amortization schedule can help you plan how high your loan payments should be.

LIFE AND CAREER SKILLS

If you have an installment loan, you'll probably be given an **amortization schedule**. That's a table showing how long it will take you to pay off your debt. It lists your payment each month for the duration of the loan. It also shows how much of each payment is being used to repay the principal versus the interest.

On the other hand, people are able to use installment loans to their advantage. By paying according to the terms of their loan agreement, they demonstrate that they're responsible, trustworthy borrowers. Such individuals build a strong credit rating that helps attract future lenders.

What else should you do to achieve the same result? Check out the final chapter for more information on the importance of using credit wisely.

REAL WORLD MATH CHALLENGE

Luke's mom needs a $9,000.00 installment loan to buy a car. She has these options:

* $9,000.00 borrowed at 6.88 percent interest for 3 years (36 months) totaling $277.40/month
* $9,000.00 borrowed at 6.97 percent interest for 5 years (60 months) totaling $178.08/month

- What would she pay in interest on each loan?
- How much more interest would she pay on the 5-year loan?

(Turn to page 30 for the answers)

BEING SMART ABOUT CREDIT

If you plan to use credit, be prepared to be an excellent record keeper! Otherwise, it's easy to lose track of how much you're spending and when payments are due. Fortunately, every time you pay for an item with your credit card, you get a receipt. Keep all of your receipts in one place. At the end of the month, you'll receive a credit card bill showing each of your charges. Check your receipts against the charges. If they don't match up, contact your credit card company immediately.

Always be aware of your balance. Remember that it's

best to pay off the balance every month, so you're not responsible for any interest charges. If you're unable to do that, then try to pay as much as you can. Even doubling or tripling the minimum required payment will help keep your balance low.

Keeping track of your receipts can help you avoid accidental charges.

It's good to start building good credit when you're young.

Finally, know what's in your credit report. Many credit agencies allow you to check your report online for a small fee. Some even let you view certain parts of your report for free. Don't forget that a wide variety of people and groups will one day view your credit report. This includes landlords and possibly future bosses. These individuals often rely on a credit report to determine if a person is reliable and responsible. If you have a lot of debt and several late payments, it's possible your credit report will reflect badly on you. Meanwhile, if you've managed your credit wisely, your report will demonstrate that you're trustworthy and capable of good decisions.

Using credit involves risks for both borrowers and lenders. But it also gives people purchasing power and often teaches them the importance of financial responsibility. Make the best choices when it comes to credit, and you'll make your credit work for you.

21ST CENTURY CONTENT

The average American adult has between two and three credit cards. These numbers are the same for most Canadian adults. In many cases, however, just one card is enough to take care of a person's purchasing needs. Using more credit cards means making more monthly payments. In turn, this makes it harder to reduce the balance on any single card.

REAL WORLD MATH CHALLENGE ANSWERS

CHAPTER TWO
Page 12
$280.15 of Mia's $500.00 credit limit remains.
$16.97 × 3 CDs = $50.91
$135.48 clothes + $19.99 sunglasses + $13.47 art supplies + $50.91 CDs = $219.85
$500.00 − $219.85 = $280.15

CHAPTER THREE
Page 19
The bike costs $481.49 total.

0.07 sales tax × $449.99 for the bike = $31.50 in sales tax
$449.99 + $31.50 = $481.49 total for the bike

It will take Patrick slightly longer than 24 weeks to repay his dad.
$481.49 ÷ $20.00 per week = 24.07 weeks

CHAPTER FOUR
Page 25
She would pay $986.40 in interest on the 3-year loan.
$277.40 per month × 36 months = $9,986.40
$9,986.40 − $9,000.00 = $986.40

She would pay $1,684.80 in interest on the 5-year loan.
$178.08 per month × 60 months = $10,684.80
$10,684.80 − $9,000.00 = $1,684.80

She would pay $698.40 more in interest on the 5-year loan.
$1,684.80 − $986.40 = $698.40

FIND OUT MORE

BOOKS

Blobaum, Cindy, and Bryan Stone (illustrator). *Explore Money! With 25 Great Projects*. White River Junction, VT: Nomad Press, 2014.

Marsico, Katie. *Money Math*. Minneapolis: Lerner Publications, 2016.

Randolph, Ryan. *How to Use Credit*. New York: PowerKids Press, 2014.

WEB SITES

Biz Kids—Credit and Debt
http://bizkids.com/themes/credit-debt
Watch online videos for a more in-depth look at how to use credit responsibly.

TheMint—Credit Card Facts
www.themint.org/kids/credit-card-facts.html
Learn more about credit cards, credit reports, and how to manage your money.

GLOSSARY

amortization schedule (ah-mur-tuh-ZAY-shuhn SKEJ-ool) a chart that shows required monthly loan payments, as well as the balance due

balance (BAL-uhns) the amount of money left unpaid on a credit card or loan

credit (KRED-it) a borrower's ability to obtain money, goods, or services with the expectation of future payment to a lender

installment loan (in-STAWL-muhnt LOHN) money borrowed typically for a large, one-time purchase and that is repaid on a monthly basis

interest (IN-trist) an amount charged for borrowing money, which is usually calculated as a percentage of the amount borrowed

mortgage (MOR-gij) a loan to buy a home or business

penalty (PEN-uhl-tee) a fee charged when an agreement is broken

principal (PRIN-suh-puhl) the unpaid balance on a loan

receipt (rih-SEET) a piece of paper showing that money, goods, mail, or a service has been received

terms (TURMZ) the conditions of an agreement or sale

trustworthy (TRUHST-wur-thee) able to be trusted and relied on to do what is right

valid (VAL-uhd) legal and able to be actively used

INDEX